W9-BJC-259

This book has been published in cooperation with Evans Publishing Group.

© Evans Brothers Limited 2010
This edition published under license from Evans Brothers Limited.

Published in the United States by
Amicus
P.O. Box 1329, Mankato, Minnesota 56002

U.S. publication copyright © 2011 Amicus. International copyright reserved in all countries.
No part of this book may be reproduced in any form without written permission from
the publisher.

Printed in China by New Era Printing Co.Ltd

Library of Congress Cataloging-in-Publication Data

Stearman, Kaye.
Travel and tourism careers / Kaye Stearman.
p. cm. -- (In the workplace)
Includes index.
Summary: "Describes jobs in the travel and tourism industry. Includes information on travel agents, tour operators, resort owners, and more, covering their responsibilities and training needed. Also includes profiles of workers in the industry"--Provided by publisher.
ISBN 978-1-60753-096-1 (library binding)
1. Tourism--Vocational guidance--Juvenile literature. I. Title.
G155.5.S74 2011
910.23--dc22

2009051727

Editor and picture researcher: Patience Coster
Designer: Guy Callaby

The author would like to thank the following for their help in producing this book: Carrie-Ann Fleming, Chris Long and Luca Neubold.

We are grateful to the following for permission to reproduce photographs: Alamy 6 (Photofusion Picture Library), 8 (Carpe Diem – France), 9 (Stock Connection Blue), 12 (David R. Frazier Photolibrary, Inc.), 13 (James Davis Photography), 14 (Adrian Sherratt), 15 (Jeff Greenberg), 16 (David Pearson), 17 (Imagebroker), 18 (Helene Rogers), 20 (A Room With Views), 21 (David R. Frazier Photolibrary, Inc.), 23 (Paul Thompson Images), 24 (Jack Sullivan), 27 (Craig Lovell/Eagle Visions Photography), 28 (Alberto Paredes), 29 (E. D. Torial), 30 (EuroStyle Graphics), 31 (Imagebroker), 34 (Eddie Gerald), 35 (Danwer Productions), 36 (Mark Downey), 37 (Glowimages RM), 38 (Directphoto.org), 39 (Directphoto.org), 43 (dbimages); Corbis 19 (Ken Seet), 25 (Gabe Palmer), 32 (Li Ziheng/xh/Xinhua Press), 33 (Ken Seet), cover and 40 (Staffan Widstrand), 41 (Robert Holmes); iStockphoto 7, 22, 26, 42.

05 10
PO1568

9 8 7 6 5 4 3 2 1

Travel AND Tourism Careers

KAYE STEARMAN

amicus
mankato, minnesota

UBERGE de JEUNESSE
YOUTH HOSTEL

Contents

	World on the Move	6
Chapter 1	**Promoting Tourism**	8
Chapter 2	**Working for a Large Company**	14
Chapter 3	**Working for a Smaller Company**	22
Chapter 4	**Getting There**	28
Chapter 5	**A Place to Stay**	34
Chapter 6	**Supporting Tourists**	40
	Further Information	44
	Glossary	45
	Index	46

World on the Move

Today's tourism industry is about much more than just travel. Tourism covers everything from older people on a day out to a family vacation at a beach resort, from a business executive on an overseas trip to a college student on a long backpacking adventure.

TYPES OF TOURISM

The travel and tourism industry is generally divided into domestic tourism and international tourism. Domestic tourism takes place within the same country and may be quite local. International tourism takes place in one or more countries.

Travel and tourism also can be divided by sector. The largest sector, employing the most people, is personal tourism—people traveling for vacations and leisure. Business travel is a smaller sector, but a higher-value one. Business travelers tend to stay in more expensive hotels and spend more than tourists.

THE GROWTH OF TOURISM

Tourism has increased a great deal over recent decades, aided by prosperity and the growth of road and air transportation. The international tourism industry is one face of globalization—the world coming together through faster communications and linked systems. People move more readily between countries for work and leisure, and one of the key factors in international tourism is visiting family members abroad. Tourism is expected to grow even more in the coming years, although economic recession is likely to mean cutbacks in some areas.

Ready to see the world—a young woman prepares for the journey of a lifetime.

Tourism may bring benefits, but it can also create pollution and waste. This beach strewn with garbage is in the Dominican Republic, a popular tourist destination in the Caribbean.

Despite its advantages, tourism can have a destructive impact. The more people travel by road and air, the more carbon emissions increase. If tourist numbers are high, they can bring about the pollution of natural treasures, the displacement of local people, and an increase in the price of food and housing. In the worst cases, tourism provides income to undemocratic and corrupt governments that exploit and cheat their own people.

CAREERS IN TOURISM

Because tourism is such a wide-ranging and ever-changing sector, you may not find it very easy to follow a defined career path. In general, large companies offer the greatest variety of jobs, travel, and locations, and the best opportunities for advancement within the company. However, many people prefer working for a smaller company or running their own business, often in a specialty or "niche" area.

For many tourism jobs, the hours are long, pay is low, and conditions are not always ideal. Jobs that involve extensive travel can be great for young, unattached people, but not for those with family commitments. Nevertheless, the skills and experience gained prove to be extremely valuable to employers and can be transferred readily into other jobs.

FINDING A JOB IN THE TRAVEL AND TOURISM INDUSTRY

Many jobs are advertised online on travel industry and company web sites. Look at the different jobs available and consider which ones best suit your skills. Consider taking a seasonal job first to give yourself a taste of the company and the industry.

Promoting Tourism

The tourism industry is big business. By spending money on food, accommodations, attractions, and souvenirs, tourists support local businesses and jobs. Some businesses would not even exist without income from visitors. But tourism can thrive only if people know what an area has to offer.

GETTING THE MESSAGE ACROSS

It is not surprising that countries, regions, cities, and towns make special efforts to attract tourists. Many have their own tourism organization. Tourism information can often be found in kiosks in downtown areas and at airports and train and bus stations. Some of these outlets just provide information, such as brochures and booklets, while others have staff who give advice or book rooms or tours.

However, this is only a small part of the promotion effort. Tourism promotion involves training and supporting businesses and staff, preparing and checking information, and undertaking advertising and media work. In other words, it is almost an industry in itself.

TO WORK IN TOURISM PROMOTION, YOU WILL NEED

- *communications skills, written and spoken*
- *a keen eye for newsworthy topics*
- *a degree or experience in journalism or public relations*

FINDING A JOB: TOURISM PROMOTION

For this job field, you need to gain experience in similar roles in other areas and have an interest in travel. It helps if you have done a bit of traveling yourself. On your resume, you should emphasize how the skills you have gained in previous work experience can transfer to travel and tourism.

This tourist office is located next to Reims Cathedral, one of France's great gothic buildings and a popular tourist attraction.

Part of the regular work in tourism promotion is calling journalists and answering inquiries.

Janet: Tourism Promotion

"I am a [promoter] for the city tourism authority. Our city is very scenic and has some beautiful and historic buildings, so we are already well known. But we can't be complacent. Tourism is a very competitive industry, and people will only come here if we can offer them good value and high standards. Although we have many tourists, they tend to come for only one or two days. We would like them to stay longer.

"I promote tourism through the media. I issue press releases and answer inquiries from journalists. I keep in touch with journalists to tell them of new developments, for example, a forthcoming exhibition or a new tourist attraction, and encourage them to feature our city in their publications. Sometimes we arrange tours for journalists or photographers.

"Last year, we had a film crew shooting scenes in the city. I know that we will benefit from the extra publicity. I hope that when moviegoers see what a great place this is, more of them will want to visit."

ONLINE TRAVEL CONSULTANTS

The Internet enables people to search and book travel online, putting together their own travel and vacation packages. But web sites also offer a valuable service by providing information for travelers, especially those seeking something unusual or different.

SEEKING INFORMATION

Perhaps tourists have an interest or hobby they want to pursue. They may be wary about food or hygiene at their vacation destination, or they may have special travel requirements. Today, there are web sites dealing with all aspects of travel, set up by tourism authorities, travel agents, and enthusiasts. Many of these web sites are interactive, enabling travelers to give their views on everything from the standard of hotel rooms and transportation and prices to the friendliness of the local people. Tourists can draw on their own experiences and add comments to the web sites, but much of the information is supplied by online travel consultants.

HANDY HINT

If you are interested in becoming a travel consultant, think about how you can improve your research skills –through reading, using the Internet, and talking to people. Work experience with a volunteer organization or charity may lead to a regular job.

MAIN TASKS: TRAVEL CONSULTANT

- *providing information by telephone, e-mail, and mail*
- *selling and sending out publications*
- *updating web site and information guides*
- *giving quotations and booking hotel rooms*
- *dealing with membership inquiries and subscriptions*
- *attending meetings and trade shows*

Electronic communication is a vital part of today's travel industry, especially for people with disabilities, who can browse information and opportunities from home or work.

Carrie-Ann: Travel Consultant

"Travel is one of my favorite things. I love the thrill of being somewhere new, full of people to meet. I enjoy the excitement of being in a strange place. But, as a wheelchair user, travel can be difficult.

"For most of my life I have traveled 'mainstream'—booking hotels through a travel agent, hobbling onto [buses], rearranging furniture to accommodate my wheelchair. It wasn't until I started working for Tourism for All that I realized travel could be made easier.

"As an information officer, my main job is to share my knowledge about all aspects of accessible tourism and travel [in my country] and overseas, from hotels to sources of [travel] funding.

"I don't only act as an information officer for wheelchair users; I also work with people with other disabilities and medical conditions. Disabled people often only need simple adjustments or a bit of extra help, but they may struggle to get people to understand what an important difference these relatively small changes can make. People with more complex needs have even more difficulties. I want to live in a world where tourism is really open to everyone."

TRAVEL AGENCIES

Travel agencies sell services to business travelers and tourists. In the twentieth century, most travel was arranged through travel agents. Today, although many people book their trips directly via the Internet, travel agents still provide an important service.

THE GROWTH OF TOURISM

With the development of mass tourism from the 1950s onward, the role of the travel agent came into its own. For the first time, most people took regular paid vacations and had the money to travel farther away from home. Travel agents offered a wide range of vacations, catering to different tastes, at prices ranging from cheap package trips to luxury vacations. They could develop itineraries; book transportation, hotels, and tours; order foreign currency, and advise travelers on matters such as visas and medical requirements.

Travel agencies operate in similar ways in most of the world—this agency is in Germany.

TO WORK AS A TRAVEL AGENT, YOU WILL NEED

- *an interest in travel, people, and places*
- *good listening and customer service skills*
- *good computer skills, for using special travel computer systems*
- *budgeting and financial knowledge*

Young backpackers sit on the deck of a ferry traveling between the Greek islands. Some may be on package tours, while others have arranged their own travel.

Travel agencies are usually commercial organizations, often part of a large company or chain, but they are also independent businesses. Many have outlets in busy shopping areas. Customers can pop in, look through brochures, and ask staff for advice. For many people, this is still the best way to arrange a vacation. They like the personal contact and the opportunity to ask questions.

A good travel agent is interested in his or her customers and willing to spend time searching for the right choice for their needs. If things go wrong, the travel agent will need to deal with customer complaints or arrange a refund or compensation payment.

THE INTERNET CHALLENGE

Today, although there are more travelers than ever before, there are fewer storefront travel agencies. This is because the Internet now provides the means for people to plan and book their travel online. Many travelers feel this gives them more control of the whole process. As a result, a lot of traditional travel agencies have closed, while others operate online or as telephone services.

Will travel agents disappear altogether? Probably not, because many people will still seek personal service and expert advice from an agent. The Internet will create many new jobs in the travel industry, especially those involving the building of web sites, search engines, and other developments.

WHERE WILL I BE?

With several years of experience working in this field, you could be managing a team of travel advisers, setting up your own travel agency, or using your travel industry skills in another customer service sector.

Working for a Large Company

There are many types of companies involved in tourism. Most are small niche operators. However, the industry is dominated by a few large companies, each with its own transportation, hotels, and tour operations.

CATERING TO DIFFERENT MARKETS

The wide range of travel brochures and travel web sites currently offered suggests that there are many different companies, each with its own name, logo, and "brand." But many of these are part of just one company or group of companies. By doing business under different names, they can cater to different sections of the market, such as family vacations, travel for young single people, or travel for older people.

Some large companies have their own chain of travel agencies or storefronts, while others sell through independent agencies or the Internet. Some specialize in one area, such as domestic or overseas travel, while others focus on package tourism.

Large companies operate under different names, each producing its own range of brochures aimed at specific markets.

A large company offers a range of jobs. Here, a tour manager on a cruise ship checks paperwork while the tourists under her charge take a sightseeing tour.

THE PROS AND CONS OF BIG BUSINESS

Large travel companies employ thousands of people at all levels, from the booking office and the airport to the travel destination. These are not just jobs that deal directly with customers; they also include support jobs in administration, finance, technology, and logistics, which underpin the company's many complex operations.

There are a lot of advantages to working in a large company. Such an organization offers a wide range of jobs and opportunities for career advancement. It runs in-house training courses. Many large companies offer benefits such as health insurance, retirement plans, and the opportunity to travel without charge or at a discounted rate. Travel reps and tour managers are provided with accommodations while they are away on work.

There are also disadvantages, however. Earnings may depend in part on commission, so the more vacations, flights, or tours staff members sell, the more they will earn. This suits some people, but not everyone enjoys the pressures of the commission system. Some people find working for a large company impersonal and unfulfilling.

Many jobs are seasonal, especially those at resorts, and are likely to appeal to younger people looking for excitement and adventure rather than those wanting a regular career path. Hours can be very long, and staff may have to work odd hours. However, despite the drawbacks, many people feel that the experience gained with a large company will support them in their future working life.

HANDY HINT

Update your resume to see what skills and experiences match the position you are applying for. Consider extra training or refresher courses to improve your skills. With a seasonal job, make sure you apply well ahead of time—most companies recruit workers many months in advance.

Goa International is one of India's largest airports, serving hundreds of thousands of package vacationers from western countries.

PACKAGE TOURISM

Package tourism is a particular type of vacation, consisting of transportation and accommodations advertised and sold together by a company. Package tourism started in the 1950s, when charter flights began taking sun-starved tourists from northern states to the beach resorts of the south.

VACATIONS MADE TO ORDER

The idea behind a package vacation is a simple one. The vacations are listed in a brochure (or today, on a web site) with their dates, travel arrangements, and prices. Prices vary according to the season, with the highest during the summer months.

Customers choose the package that best suits their needs: for example, facilities for children for a family vacation, sports activities and a lively nightlife for young, single people, and a quiet, relaxed atmosphere for older groups.

WINTER SPORTS

Package vacations are not confined to beach resorts. Winter sports, especially skiing, make up an enormous seasonal industry at resorts in mountain areas. Many winter sports vacations are sold as packages, with the company organizing travel, food, and lodging, often in a chalet or guesthouse. There are a large number of jobs available, including chalet hosts, ski instructors, child-care providers, drivers, and resort managers.

Many employees are local people, but others come from outside the area for the winter season. Chalet hosts are based in the chalet and look after 8 to 12 guests each, preparing breakfasts and evening meals, cleaning up, and dealing with any problems that arise.

The big attraction of the job for many chalet hosts is that most of their day is left free for skiing. Wages are not high, but companies provide accommodations and food, and they often include free ski lift passes, equipment rental, and medical insurance.

TO WORK AS A CHALET HOST, YOU WILL NEED

- ***good and varied cooking skills***
- ***an ability to deliver high-quality customer service***
- ***a mature and well-organized approach to your job***
- ***a hardworking temperament***
- ***a willingness to work long hours***

Winter sports are a major industry in mountain resorts. These children are being taught by a ski instructor in a beginner course at a ski school in Austria.

IN THE RESORT

Resort representatives (reps for short) play a key role in package tourism, supporting and assisting tourists with information and advice.

There are several types of resort employees, including customer service representatives, activity directors, and transportation coordinators. There are also specialty roles, including children's activity directors, overseas entertainers, and resort managers, who ensure that the operation runs smoothly.

Working as a resort rep can be great fun, but it is also hard work and takes the rep away from his or her home and family for months at a time. Many resort reps are young—the average age is 25—and work for only a few seasons. Others continue longer, perhaps moving into an administrative or managerial role in the resort or in the company's office.

TO WORK AS A RESORT REP, YOU WILL NEED

- *appropriate qualifications—for example, child-care qualifications to work as a children's activity director*
- *some work experience—customer service or sales is useful*
- *a friendly and approachable manner*
- *to be calm under pressure*
- *math skills—you will be selling tours and dealing with currency*
- *flexibility*
- *a willingness to work long hours*

Many vacation resorts, like this one in Menorca, Spain, put on special entertainment events for children. Here, a children's activity director joins in the fun at a mini-disco.

A current passport, complete with necessary visas, is essential for most international travel. Immigration officials and check-in staff need to check passports, while hotel staff may also require passport details.

Tracey: Resort Rep

"As a [resort] rep, my work is organized around a weekly cycle, with the busiest period being 'changeover day.' Flights arrive and depart in the early morning. We take departing guests to the airport and direct the new arrivals to the [bus]. After a head count, we set off to the resort, which is an hour away. On the trip in, I introduce myself to the guests.

"We drop guests off at their hotels. After the last drop-off, I get a few hours of sleep and a quick breakfast before heading to our base hotel for my first welcome meeting.

"I talk to the guests about the resort and the facilities and hand out information leaflets. I sell excursions and recommend cafés and restaurants. I deal with any complaints—these tend to be about unsuitable rooms or missing luggage. Then it's on to the next welcome meeting. It's a long day, and we finish with a party for guests at a local bar. Luckily, most days aren't quite so long.

"In the high season and [during] school [breaks], I am responsible for between 70 and 90 guests; in the low season there are far fewer. The main thing is to be available when needed. Some people need a lot of attention, while others I hardly see at all. I enjoy my job, despite the pressure!"

FLIGHT BOOKING SPECIALISTS

Some large companies specialize in selling airfares, rather than package vacations. Many look like traditional travel agencies with offices in big cities and with telephone booking services; others operate only though the Internet.

LONG-HAUL FLIGHTS

Most of these companies sell long-haul flights, which usually go to another continent, such as Europe or Asia. When it comes to buying expensive long-haul flight tickets, some tourists prefer to discuss their plans with a travel agent and explain exactly what they are looking for regarding dates, routes, destinations, and prices.

Some flight booking services buy up blocks of airline seats and sell them at lower prices than other agencies. They may be the first to know about special offers or new routes. If price is not the main consideration, they can look for more convenient options, such as flights that leave or arrive during the daytime rather than at night, or journeys with interesting or unusual routes. Flight specialists often book hotels or create packages to suit individual travelers.

MAIN TASKS: FLIGHT BOOKING SPECIALIST

- *communicating with customers face-to-face, on the telephone, and through e-mail*
- *finding flights and accommodations to suit customer requirements*
- *making reservations, ticketing, calculating, and collecting payments*
- *keeping up-to-date with airline information, prices, and taxes*
- *advising customers on travel, visa, and medical requirements*

Long-haul flights to tourist destinations are an important sector of the travel industry.

Good geographical knowledge is vital for staff working in the travel industry.

David: Flight Booking Specialist

"I work at a large travel [agency] with offices in Europe, Australia, and North America. We specialize in long-haul flights, although we also sell short flights and weekend breaks. We open six days a week on a shift system starting at 8 A.M. and finishing at 7 P.M.

"My customers are a mixture of young backpackers who want cheaper flights and generally don't mind [inconvenient] or long transit times, and older, more affluent people who are willing to pay more for convenience and will often book hotels and tours as well as flights.

"I deal both with walk-in customers and telephone customers—it can be quite difficult juggling the calls. You have to be a good listener and pay attention to detail. You need to check names, prices, special requirements, insurance, visas, and health requirements. Often, I reserve a flight, so a customer can come back to book later. Most people book by credit card—it gives them better protection if something goes wrong.

"You have to be a traveler to do this job well, and all the [agents] here have traveled on at least two continents. We enjoy using our own experience to help other travelers."

Working for a Smaller Company

Although large companies cater to the majority of people, most travel agencies are small and medium-sized companies. They do well because they can offer tailored services aimed at particular groups, using expertise based on their own knowledge, contacts, and experience.

SMALL COMPANIES

The simplest type of company is a business owned by just one person, providing a limited number of services. More common is a business partnership (two or more people who are joint owners) or a company with between 3 and 10 staff members. Employees often work on a part-time or seasonal basis, with the owners joining in carrying out the business.

Many businesses stay small either because their market is limited or simply because they prefer it that way. The owners may have started the business because they are interested in a particular country or area, interest, or hobby. They know their customers well and can provide a friendly and personal service.

A small company can offer a range of activities, such as kayaking, in a quiet location far from the bustle of the crowded resorts.

A camping or motorhome trip offers a different sort of break. This campsite is in northern Italy.

MEDIUM-SIZED COMPANIES

Some businesses increase in size to meet growing demand. Most still specialize but broaden their appeal by adding new services, activities, accommodations, or tours, or by extending into new areas or countries. For example, a company providing walking tours may start to offer tours in other areas or add other activities, such as mountain biking or kayaking. The operators may decide to offer a greater range of accommodations, for example, at luxury hotels or campsites.

As a company grows, it will need to employ more staff and find more financing, either in the form of loans or by bringing in extra business partners. Eventually, the business may grow so large that the owners decide to sell it to a larger company.

GETTING WORK

Finding a job with a small company is not always easy. Some are family businesses and rarely employ extra staff. If they do, it may be by word of mouth or personal recommendation.

A medium-sized company, employing between 10 and 50 people, will recruit in a more formal way, through classified ads, the Internet, or employment agencies, and will look for specific qualifications or experience. There is more opportunity for career advancement in a medium-sized company.

TO WORK FOR A SMALL COMPANY, YOU WILL NEED

- ***good communication skills***
- ***a flexible and adaptable personality***
- ***a thorough and precise approach to your work***
- ***a willingness to learn on the job***
- ***an interest in travel and the area of specialization***

REACHING OUT TO CUSTOMERS

To survive in the competitive tourism sector, specialty tour operators have to market their services to potential clients. Unlike large companies, they cannot afford big-budget television advertising, and they are more likely to use brochures and web sites. However, often the most effective marketing is based on recommendations by satisfied customers.

MARKETING MATERIALS

Brochures are important marketing tools for most travel agencies, large or small. A good brochure should attract potential customers with interesting text and illustrations while providing essential information, such as travel dates and prices. Putting together a good brochure takes painstaking research and attention to detail.

Today, most travel agencies have their own web sites. Sometimes a web site replaces the traditional travel brochure, but often it is provided in addition to a brochure. Unlike brochures, web sites are not limited by space or printing costs and can be updated easily. Many agencies send regular e-mail bulletins to customers who sign up on their web sites.

MAIN TASKS: MARKETING DIRECTOR

- *developing a timetable and budget*
- *approving the design of brochures and other materials*
- *assembling and checking information*
- *writing text and sourcing photos*
- *editing text and making sure it relates to the photos*
- *organizing the printing and distribution of the brochure to customers*

Travel brochures are displayed at a travel agency. The brochure is a vital marketing tool for small companies.

The growing numbers of retired people with extra leisure time are an important market for the travel industry.

Kate: Marketing Director

"I work for a business that arranges [vacations] for older people. My most important task is to write our annual brochure. This is sent to thousands of regular customers and distributed to potential clients at meetings and exhibitions.

"The brochure must contain essential information about our [vacation sites] and their facilities, together with theme weeks and price lists. We want each brochure to look different from the last, refreshing the design and using new text and photos. We operate on a strict budget, so it can't be too extravagant.

"This year, I began by holding informal meetings with some regular customers to see what they liked and disliked about our previous brochures. They told us that they wanted more information about our facilities and clearer details on prices. They also said the photos were too gloomy! So I have used their feedback to make changes this year, including cheerful photos.

"Overall, everything went very smoothly. The worst part is checking that all the dates and prices are correct. The last days are frantic, and I heave a sigh of relief when the brochure goes to the printers and then on to the customers."

SPECIALTY OPERATORS

Look through the travel pages of a newspaper or on the Internet, and you will find advertisements for a huge variety of vacations. Specialty or hobby magazines will feature travel operators catering to your interest. There are vacations for noisy steam train enthusiasts and for silent birdwatchers, for energetic mountain bikers and for relaxed yoga practitioners. Maybe you want an ecotour on an organic farm or a guided hike across a mountain range. What about a luxury guided safari, or perhaps you'd prefer a road trip with your own motorhome? Whatever your preference, there will be a travel operator who can offer just what you want.

Mountain biking is a relatively new area of activity. Some specialty companies arrange food, accommodations, and luggage transportation for their guests.

FINDING A JOB: TOUR OPERATOR

Search through specialty web sites and magazines and contact companies in areas where you have an interest. Build up relevant personal or work experience in travel, for example, as a guide or tour manager.

WHERE WILL I BE?

In a small company, there are opportunities to take the initiative and quickly add to your skills. You could soon become a team leader in the office or, if you are interested in the activities side of the operation, you could be a guide or expedition leader. Ultimately, you could end up running your own business.

Accompanied by a local guide, a tourist enjoys meeting a llama at Lauca National Park, Chile.

Luca: Travel Operator and Manager

"I am the director of Llama Travel, a company that specializes in guided [tours] in Latin America. I founded the company seven years ago with a colleague. At first, Llama Travel operated solely in Peru, a country I know well. As the company grew, we added new destinations in Ecuador, Chile, and Argentina. Our aim is to offer good-value, interesting tours in a socially responsible way that benefits customers and local people.

"Today, Llama Travel has around 2,000 customers a year and employs nine staff in its London office. Staff responsibilities fall into three main areas: communicating with customers, usually by telephone or e-mail; communicating with suppliers (airlines, hotels, etc.); and company administration, including finance or [technology]. While most staff focus on set tasks, it is important that they can do a variety of jobs.

"When recruiting staff, I look for experience in Latin America, together with the appropriate skills. On a personal level, a staff member must be well-organized, have good [computer] skills, be flexible, and be able to communicate with customers and suppliers. I encourage staff to contribute to the company by developing new destinations and services.

"My job is to oversee the business as a whole and ensure that it is financially stable and meeting our business objectives. It is much more than a nine-to-five job. I find it very satisfying to know that we have built a company based around my knowledge and love of Latin America."

Getting There

People travel to their destinations in many different ways. Some use their own vehicles, especially for shorter distances or if they have a lot of luggage. But millions of travelers rely on mass transportation, such as trains, buses, ferries, ships, or planes.

TRAINS AND BUSES

Good transportation facilities and services are vital to tourism. Not only do they transport millions of people to their destinations, but they also are an industry in their own right and employ staff at all levels of the transportation chain.

We all know of the frontline staff —from the ticket sellers and information staff at stations and booking offices, to the onboard staff such as drivers, guards, stewards, and ticket inspectors, who operate our trains and buses. But behind these groups are the largely hidden backroom staff. They inspect and maintain the vehicles, equipment, and facilities and operate the complex systems that run and monitor the transportation networks. Many of these jobs are highly technical and require specific qualifications and special training, through on-the-job training or tech school or college courses.

A train is cleaned at the main station of Madrid, Spain's capital city.

Passengers expect good food and service when on a pleasure cruise. Here, waiters remove used dishes as passengers relax on the sun deck while cruising on the Danube River in Europe.

TRAVELING BY WATER

In some areas, for example, around Washington's Puget Sound or the Great Lakes, ferries are an important means of transportation. In general, these are fairly short trips, sometimes only a few hours. However, because ferries can carry hundreds of passengers, they have many onboard services, including catering, retail, and entertainment, all of which offer job opportunities.

Cruise ships provide a different type of service—a vacation afloat. A cruise may last from a few days to several months, but most cruises last two or three weeks. With ferries, the main aim is to get passengers to their destination quickly and in reasonable comfort, but with cruise ships, the focus is on visiting scenic destinations and providing entertainment and high levels of service. A large cruise ship may have hundreds of passengers and an equal number of crew and service personnel. However, many of these jobs are filled by professional cabin crew on long-term contracts, and the opportunities for casual or seasonal work are limited.

FINDING A JOB: IN THE TRANSPORTATION INDUSTRY

Think about whether you are willing to work shifts or spend periods of time away from home. Research the different jobs available and the requirements needed. Consider any internships and in-house training offered.

AIR TRAVEL

Without air travel, the tourism industry would be very different. People would not be able to travel quickly and safely to vacation destinations far from their homes. Thousands of tourism businesses—hotels and guest houses, cafés and restaurants, guide services, and tour companies—would not exist.

CONTROVERSIAL ISSUES

Air travel is a controversial subject. Supporters say it is vital to the world economy, playing an important part in global business and tourism. Critics argue that planes are a major source of carbon emissions, which contribute to global warming. They also say that communities situated near airports suffer because of the noise and traffic pollution airports produce.

What is not in dispute is that airlines and airports employ large numbers of people. For example, in 2008, Atlanta's Hartsfield-Jackson International Airport, the world's busiest international airport with 90 million passengers a year, employed 56,000 people.

TO WORK AT AN AIRPORT, YOU WILL NEED

- *good teamwork skills*
- *a strong customer focus*
- *an awareness of safety issues*
- *a thorough and precise approach to your work*
- *quick reactions, to cope with unexpected situations or emergencies*
- *to pass a criminal background check*

Los Angeles International Airport in California offers both national and international flights and is one of the world's busiest transportation hubs.

One of the greatest tests of an airport is its capacity to unload and transfer passenger luggage quickly and securely.

JOBS AT THE AIRPORT

Large airports offer a huge variety of jobs. These include management, information technology, security and safety services, engineering, maintenance and transportation crew (both on land and in air), and retail staff in shops and services. In addition, there are staff who work for individual airlines, or for independent companies that handle business for several airlines.

Some jobs, such as airline pilot and air traffic controller, are highly technical and require specific training. Other jobs vital to airport operations include loading and handling baggage and freight, helping to move aircraft to the right place for refueling, and assisting in airfield maintenance. Many of these roles require experience gained from apprenticeships and on-the-job training. Others are more customer-focused, such as check-in staff or customer service agents.

Working at an airport does not suit everyone. Airports operate long hours—often around the clock—and many staff work in shifts, perhaps starting in the early hours or ending late at night, or on different days each week. However, many employees maintain that shift work is convenient and suits their personal or family needs.

Journalists from home and abroad gather to examine the security procedures at the new international airport in Beijing, China, before the 2008 Olympic Games.

LANDSIDE AND AIRSIDE

Airports are divided into "landside"—the reception area open to everyone—and "airside"—the area open only to passengers who have passed through security and passport controls. Some staff work only landside, but many have to pass from one area to another every day.

Airports work with strict schedules and are very security conscious. Staff receive training in safety and undertake security drills. They are expected to be disciplined and alert at all times. Strict timing and good teamwork are important, as one delayed plane can cause problems at the airport for hours afterward.

WHERE WILL I BE?

Experience as a member of an airport's check-in staff may lead to a position as a check-in supervisor, managing a team.

MAIN TASKS: AIRPORT CHECK-IN STAFF

- ***checking passenger identification and tickets***
- ***allocating seats***
- ***ensuring passengers know their boarding time and gate***
- ***implementing security procedures***
- ***ensuring help for disabled passengers and others who need special assistance***
- ***checking passenger information at the boarding gate***

Anita: Airport Check-in Worker

"I work at the check-in for a company that provides services for several foreign airlines. One day I may be dealing with business passengers bound for Asia, and the next day with tourists headed for a beach resort.

"Many people think check-in is straightforward, but our tasks can be complex. We need both [computer] and customer skills. Check-in counters open two or three hours before the flight is scheduled to depart and close 45 minutes before takeoff. Sometimes lines build up, but we try to keep people calm and ensure the process moves along smoothly.

"We make sure the name on the passport [or ID] matches that on the ticket and see that the passport and any visas are in order. We allocate seats and check that luggage conforms to size and weight restrictions. We ask passengers standard security questions, such as whether they have packed their luggage themselves and whether anyone has asked them to carry extra items. Then we [attach] tags to the luggage so that it can be routed through to the destination.

"Each day brings different problems. For example, one passenger's visa only became valid a day after her flight was scheduled to arrive, so I had to reschedule her connecting flight for the following day. Several passengers were delayed and were checked in at the last minute.

"After check-in closes, I go airside to the departure gate. We double-check passports and boarding passes. We oversee boarding, making sure that older and disabled people, and families with young children, board first. Our task is complete when all passengers have boarded and the flight is ready to depart."

Check-in at the airport—friendly efficiency is key to smooth service.

A Place to Stay

Business travelers and vacationers alike say that one of their top priorities is accommodations that meet their needs. Whether they seek a luxury hotel, a chain motel, a hostel, or a beach hut, travelers expect their accommodations to be safe, clean, comfortable, convenient, and a good value for their money.

TYPES OF ACCOMMODATIONS

Large cities offer many types of accommodations. In smaller towns or in rural areas, the choice is more limited, but prices are generally lower.

Chain hotels in large cities have the most rooms. These hotels are usually graded by the standard of facilities and services they offer—ranging from five-star luxury to the more basic two- or three-star establishments. Three- and four-star hotels are aimed at the business market, though many tourists stay in these, too. "Boutique" hotels are smaller luxury hotels with a more individual feel.

One- and two-star hotels tend to be smaller family-run hotels or bed-and-breakfasts (B&Bs), although these often have their own

A luxury hotel in Alexandria, Egypt, caters to business travelers and tourists.

TO WORK IN A HOTEL, YOU WILL NEED

- *to be good at customer relations*
- *a calm, professional manner*
- *a professional appearance, especially in front-desk jobs*
- *good computer skills—especially Windows, Excel, and reservations systems*
- *financial and budgeting skills*
- *good teamwork skills*
- *to be good at time management*
- *a willingness to work odd hours*

A waiter knocks on a hotel room door as he delivers a room service meal order.

separate rating system. Motels are aimed at travelers who want a convenient room at a modest price. Many motels are situated close to highways or airports, and some even have self-service check-in. Hostels are another budget alternative—they usually have some shared facilities and are generally aimed at younger travelers.

WORKING IN A HOTEL

Hotel chains offer many employment opportunities at different levels. For every staff member "front-of-house" (directly dealing with guests), there are many more backroom jobs. Increasingly, these jobs require special training and good computer skills; these qualities are especially useful for work dealing with reservations and payments. As with many other jobs in travel and tourism, hours can be long and sometimes inconvenient.

Hotel chains usually offer in-house training and the opportunity to follow a career within the company. In a smaller hotel or hostel, work is likely to be less rigid, and there is more opportunity to try out different roles. However, wages will probably be lower, jobs are more likely to be seasonal or part-time, and career opportunities are limited.

HOTEL CHAINS

Most hotel chains belong to large companies that own hotels in many states. As with package tourism, one company may have several hotel chains, each with a different name and brand, catering to different markets.

Hotel chains aim to offer the same standard of facilities and service at each hotel, wherever it is located. This means the guests should know exactly what to expect. Business travelers especially appreciate this environment, as it offers no surprises and allows them to stay and work in a familiar atmosphere.

MAINTAINING STANDARDS

Staff working for a hotel chain are expected to maintain certain standards of appearance and behavior and are given in-house training to ensure these are maintained. Staff members are issued uniforms to reflect their jobs and name badges so they can be easily identified. In return, those who do well have the opportunity to learn different roles and be promoted within the company.

MAIN TASKS: FRONT-DESK WORK

- ***recording reservations and cancellations***
- ***checking in guests and allocating rooms***
- ***keeping tabs and processing bills***
- ***checking out guests and collecting payment***
- ***dealing with sales and currency exchanges***
- ***dealing with requests, inquiries, and complaints***

Hotel staff at a luxury hotel in Asia enjoy a moment of relaxation before guests arrive.

Front-of-house staff provide round-the-clock service to guests.

Jamal: Assistant Night Manager

"I have worked for a leading hotel chain for five years. I started doing shift work as a student and got so interested in the hotel business that I decided that was where I wanted to work.

"For personal reasons, night work suits me. I worked for several years as a night auditor, managing the till and bill payments. The next step was as a reception shift leader, managing a small team. Last year, I was promoted to assistant night manager.

"The night team takes over after the daytime management team leaves. We are there to keep all the services running smoothly. Some people think it must be easy work, but a lot can happen at night.

"Friday and Saturday nights are the busiest. Our banquet rooms host parties and wedding receptions, and guests often stay at the hotel, so people are going to and from the different areas most of the night. Generally, it is just high spirits, but sometimes things get rowdy—people may drink too much, or fights may break out, so we have to be ready to intervene.

"People also lose things—including their room keys—and some forget their room numbers. It's a matter of being tactful and diplomatic while keeping an eye out for any trouble that might develop. Safety and security have to be our number one priority."

HOSTEL LIFE

Not everyone wants or needs to stay in hotels. Many budget travelers choose to stay in cheaper accommodations, such as hostels, bed-and-breakfasts (B&Bs), or in family homes, often called homestays.

YOUTH HOSTELS

The largest group of hostels, generally known as youth hostels, belongs to Hostelling International. Youth hostels started in Germany in 1909 to provide affordable accommodations for students on walking vacations. Today, there are 90 youth hostel associations operating 4,500 hostels in 80 countries. Despite their name, most cater to people of all ages.

Youth hostels employ many young people on a seasonal basis, and some employees go on to build careers in hostel management.

Youth hostels like this one in Paris, France, provide budget accommodations for travelers and cater mainly to young backpackers.

TO BE A GENERAL ASSISTANT IN A YOUTH HOSTEL, YOU WILL NEED

- *to be over 18 (most applicants are between ages 18 and 25)*
- *common sense and an open, cheerful personality*
- *practical work experience, especially in housekeeping or catering*
- *to attend youth-hostel-run open days for practical assessment tests*
- *to pass police and other child safety checks*

WHERE WILL I BE?

If you move up the career ladder in youth hostel work, you could rise to become a hostel warden. The experience gained from working in hostels will also qualify you for a hotel management post, or you could take the plunge and try running your own hotel or guesthouse.

Many youth hostels provide meals for their guests, and some also let travelers use their kitchen facilities.

Chris: General Assistant, Youth Hostel

"I am a general assistant at a youth hostel deep in the countryside. My day starts at 7 A.M., when we unlock the hostel and prepare breakfasts for guests. If we have a school party staying, it can be really noisy. We check out departing guests and then spend the morning washing, cleaning, and doing routine maintenance.

"The afternoon is usually free, but I have to be back by 5 P.M. to reopen the hostel. I check in new guests and allocate available rooms to them. The staff all pitch in preparing the evening meals—sometimes it's just for a few people, other times it's a full house. Once we have done the cleaning up, I often join the guests for a chat.

"The job has two main attractions for me. I love the countryside, especially as I am a keen birdwatcher. And I really enjoy meeting new people. Although we are a small hostel, we get visitors from all over the world. It really inspires me to travel myself.

"The downside is that the job is seasonal, normally eight or nine months a year, and the wages are not high. But accommodation and food are included, and I can save quite a lot of my salary. It's great experience, and a lot of trust is placed in you. As a general assistant, you have to be very responsible and prepared to [help out with] anything, but I don't mind—it makes life more challenging."

Supporting Tourists

While some tourists prefer to relax or party, others are eager to explore their new surroundings. While some are happy to use the wide range of guidebooks available, others prefer to rely on the expertise of a guide. There are many types of guides, and their jobs are often seasonal. Tour managers tend to be employed to look after clients as part of their vacation package.

ENTERTAINING WORK

Tour guide jobs are available at theme parks, amusement parks, zoos, and similar visitor attractions. Here, the principal roles are service-oriented, for example, helping customers, managing lines, and entertaining children. Although these jobs can be quite low level, they provide experience and may lead to more permanent positions.

Some tours and cruises provide guides, generally called tour managers, as part of the tour package. Other companies hire guides locally or recommend guides they know to be reliable. In many tourist destinations, guides offer their services directly to tourists, sometimes amid fierce competition for business.

Ecotourism is a growing sector of the tourist market. These tourists are looking for chimpanzees in the trees of Uganda's Kibale Forest.

A local tour guide with tourists in the French Quarter of New Orleans, Louisiana.

TOUR GUIDES

Tour guides are based locally and offer a variety of services. The simplest format is where a guide recites a standard commentary on a tour bus or boat. However, good guides will provide a much more comprehensive service, tailoring each tour to the interests and capacities of their audience, answering questions, and knowing what aspects appeal to different age groups and nationalities.

Walking tours, led by an expert guide, are popular in many cities. These take place at fixed times and usually last between one and three hours, with between 3 and 15 people in each group. Walking tours tend to focus on a particular area or special interest (for example, historic churches, literary life, industrial remains, or "hidden history").

It is not easy to become an accredited guide in a major city such as London, Paris, or New York. Guides need to be well-educated and knowledgeable about a range of subjects, including history, art, and architecture. Often, they need certification from the local tourism authority. Guides have to be well-spoken, articulate, and able to deal with different groups of people with tact and humor.

Guides also need stamina to guide people in all weather. Not surprisingly, most guides are older people who become guides after successful careers in education, archaeology, or even show business.

MAIN TASKS: TOUR GUIDE

- ***assembling the group and assessing various people's needs***
- ***collecting payment***
- ***leading the group and keeping the tour on time***
- ***giving a lively commentary and answering questions***
- ***dealing tactfully but firmly with any difficulties***

A tour group hikes on the Perito Moreno glacier, Argentina, led by an expert tour guide.

MAKING A TRIP MEMORABLE

Good guides do much more than simply show people the sights—they will make the tourist experience memorable. The visitors leave feeling they have learned something new and interesting or seen familiar sights with new eyes.

TOUR MANAGERS

A tour manager is much more than just a guide. Tour managers (sometimes called couriers or escorts) are employed by the tour operator. In many ways, their role is similar to that of a resort representative, except that they are not based in one resort and are constantly on call.

Tour managers travel and eat with their group and stay at the same hotels. The tour manager is in charge of the group's well-being throughout the trip, ensuring that travel is safe, that accommodations and food reach quality standards, and that customers receive what they pay for. The tour manager solves any problems that arise. If a guest falls ill or is injured, the tour manager makes sure the guest receives good medical attention, even if it means arranging for him or her to return home.

WHERE WILL I BE?

If the idea of becoming a tour guide appeals to you, it may well be that it suits your independent and freewheeling temperament. You could continue your career as a freelancer, choosing when to work, or you could end up running your own travel agency.

TO BE A TOUR MANAGER, YOU WILL NEED

- ***extensive travel experience, including difficult environments***
- ***a college degree in a related field (for example, geography or history)***
- ***a friendly and approachable personality***
- ***organizational, time management, and administrative skills***
- ***knowledge of, or fluency in, foreign languages***
- ***to be in good health, with lots of stamina***

Anton: Tour Manager

"I have worked as an adventure tour manager for three years. At the moment, I am based in Vietnam. I escort each group from the time they arrive to their departure two weeks later.

"Adventure travel is different from the usual escorted tour. Rather than just sightseeing, people sign up for an active [vacation]. So we go kayaking in Ha Long Bay, [hiking] in the Sapa Mountains, rafting on the Red River, and riding elephants through the jungle, all with local guides.

"After breakfast, I collect the group and we go by [bus] to our destination. I have briefed them the night before on what to expect and what to take—protective clothing, insect repellent, and so on. After a morning hike past paddy fields and a visit to a local temple, we have lunch by the riverbank. Then we go by boat downstream to the village for our overnight stay. People have time to relax or explore before dinner and a display of local dancing.

"When I tell people about my job, they think it must one long vacation—but being responsible for people's safety and welfare is no holiday, believe me! I also have to do a lot of paperwork, such as daily reports, accounts, and incident sheets. Travelers pay good money for their tours, so they want every day to be interesting and memorable."

The experience of a lifetime—tourists take an elephant ride in Laos.

Further Information

BOOKS

Burns, Jennifer Bobrow. *Career Opportunities in Travel and Hospitality.* Ferguson, 2010.

Cohn, Jessica. *Travel and Transportation.* Ferguson, 2009.

Eberts, Marjorie, Linda Brothers, and Ann Gisler. *Careers in Travel, Tourism, and Hospitality.* McGraw-Hill, 2006.

Espeja, Roman (ed.). *What Is the Impact of Tourism?* Greenhaven Press, 2009.

Ferguson's Careers in Focus: Travel and Hospitality. Ferguson, 2007.

Inskipp, Carol. *Travel and Tourism.* Smart Apple Media, 2009.

Solway, Andrew. *Sustainable Tourism.* Arcturus Publishing, 2010.

WEB SITES

www.bls.gov/oco
For hundreds of different types of jobs—such as those in the travel industry—the Occupational Outlook Handbook gives information on education needed, earnings, job prospects, and more.

www.careeroverview.com/travel-agent-careers.html
This site offers an overview of travel agent careers, travel agent training and job qualifications, employment opportunities, and earnings information.

www.hihostels.com
This site is for Hostelling International, which includesYouth Hostel Associations worldwide.

www.hiusa.org
Learn about Hostelling International USA and get a glimpse of the job opportunities available at hostels nationwide.

www.sustainabletravelinternational.org
The future of travel is green, fair, and responsible. Learn what one nonprofit is doing internationally to promote responsible travel, and what opportunities exist for those interested in working in this field.

www.wttc.org
The site of the World Travel & Tourism Council, a forum for chief executives of the world's 100 leading businesses in the travel and tourism industry, which includes statistics on tourism worldwide.

Glossary

accessible when something is designed so that it can be used by disabled people, for example, ramps or wide doors for wheelchair users

apprenticeship a period of time, often several years, during which a person combines work with on-the-job and other training to qualify for a particular job (usually for younger people)

background check an official check to see if a potential employee has a police record that might bar him or her from certain types of employment, for example, work with children or vulnerable people

backroom jobs jobs that do not deal directly with the public

brand the "identity" of a company—a brand includes things such as company name, logo, and image

brochure a booklet with text and images outlining what a travel operator is offering its customers (for example, tours and hotels)

carbon emissions carbon dioxide outputs caused by activities such as burning fossil fuels, deforestation, and vehicle exhaust

chain a number of hotels and agencies with the same name and brand, owned by one company

commission payment made according to results, rather than as wage or salary

communications skills skills involving the ability to get your message across to others, usually through speaking or writing

compensation money paid to a customer or guests to make up for faulty goods or bad service

disability a physical handicap or learning difficulty that means a person may need some extra support to participate equally in society

ecotour a tourist venture that claims to aid the local environment or to have little or no adverse impact on the environment

exhibition a meeting where companies can exhibit their goods and services

frontline jobs jobs dealing directly with the public

front-of-house the first point of contact with the public, for example, the job of hotel receptionist

homestay staying as a paying guest in a family home

hostel a less expensive alternative to a hotel

insurance By taking out insurance, a person pays to protect against risk and receive compensation in case of injury or accident.

itinerary a travel schedule

logistics developing, following, and monitoring systems

logo an identifying symbol that is part of a company's brand

long-haul flights long flights between continents, usually lasting more than five hours

marketing bringing a product or service to the public, for example, through advertising or mailing a brochure

package vacation a vacation where the tour operator provides travel, transfers, accommodations, and sometimes food as part of a travel package for a set price

quality standards agreed standards of service and presentation, for example, of rooms, facilities, and food

partnership two or more people running a company

passport a document of nationality, usually needed for international travel

press release a short document issued by a company, usually to announce news or promote a new product or service

refund a repayment to a customer who returns goods or cancels a service

representative/rep the representative of a travel operator or company whose main job is to look after a group of customers or guests

reservation an agreement to reserve a room or flight for a guest or customer

seasonal work work that is available only at certain times of year

socially responsible tourism tourism based upon ethical principles; these might include a promise not to pollute or destroy the environment, or to support local employment

suppliers companies that supply goods or services, for example, hotels and airlines

visa a stamp or document in a passport that allows the passport holder to travel in a certain country

Index

adventure travel 43
advertisements 8, 24, 26
airports 30, 31, 32, 33
air travel 30

backpackers 21
bed-and-breakfast (B&B) 34, 38
brands 14, 36
brochures 13, 14, 16, 24, 25
buses 28
business partnerships 22, 36
business travel 6, 34, 36

carbon emissions 7, 30
chalet host 17
check-in staff 19, 31, 32, 33
children's activity director 18
commission system 15
cruise ship 29

disability 11
domestic tourism 6

economic recession 6
ecotourism 26

ferries 29
flight booking services 20, 21

globalization 6
guides (tourist and tour) 40, 41, 42, 43

hostels 35, 38, 39
hotels 34, 35, 36, 37

information provider 10, 11
in-house training 15, 35
international tourism 6
Internet 10, 12, 13, 14, 23, 26

Latin America 27
long-haul flights 20, 21

marketing director 24, 25
motels 35

night manager 37

online travel consultant 10

package holidays 12, 16, 18
personal tourism 6
pollution 7, 30
promoting tourism 8, 9

resort reps 15, 18, 19

seasonal jobs 7, 15, 35, 39
ski vacations 17
specialty tour operators 26
support jobs 15, 28, 30, 31, 35

tourism promotion 8, 9
tourist information organizations 8, 10
tour manager 15, 42, 43
trains 28

travel agents and travel agencies 10, 12, 13, 14, 20, 21

Vietnam 43

web sites 7, 10, 13, 16, 24
wheelchair users 11
winter sports 17

youth hostels 38, 39